LANDSCAPE
ESSENTIALS

CREATIVE
PUBLISHING
international

MINNETONKA, MINNESOTA

Credits

Copyright © 1996
Creative Publishing International, Inc.
5900 Green Oak Drive
Minnetonka, Minnesota 55343
1-800-328-3895
All rights reserved
Printed in U.S.A.

President: Iain Macfarlane

Created by: The Editors of Creative Publishing International, Inc., in cooperation with Black & Decker. ⬛ BLACK&DECKER is a trademark of the Black & Decker Corporation and is used under license.

Printed on American paper by:
 Quebecor Printing
 02 01 00 99 98 / 5 4 3 2

Books available in this series:

Wiring Essentials
Plumbing Essentials
Carpentry Essentials
Painting Essentials
Flooring Essentials
Landscape Essentials
Masonry Essentials
Door & Window Essentials
Roof System Essentials
Deck Essentials
Porch & Patio Essentials
Built-In Essentials

NOTICE TO READERS

Contents

Plan ahead and be patient when designing your new landscape. Remember that plants grow and spread, and stone and wood structures change appearance as they weather. Landscape designers say that it takes at least five years for a landscape to reach its finished look. In the landscape shown above (inset), the owner chose to plant a few well-spaced shrubs and perennials. Several years later (larger photo), this attractive yard is approaching maturity without being overcrowded.

Landscape Planning

Designing and building a successful landscape begins with an understanding of your needs and goals. The purpose can be as simple as improving the appearance of a home by adding a flower garden or as complex as reshaping the entire yard with retaining walls to eliminate erosion. But in any good landscape, the design addresses specific problems and goals. A landscape plan that incorporates these goals will help you accomplish your projects more easily.

A detailed landscape plan takes time to develop, but helps ensure smooth work and successful results. Your finished plans should include detailed drawings, an accurate budget, a list of materials, and a realistic time schedule.

Evaluate your existing landscape carefully as you begin to plan. To save money and time, plan the new landscape so it makes use of existing features that are both attractive and functional—a favorite flower garden, a garden walk, or a healthy tree, for example. You can transplant many hardy bushes and most perennial flowers from one part of your yard to another to fit a new landscape plan.

Although most of the projects shown in this book can be done without a work permit, always check with the local inspections office before you begin. If a building permit is required, you will need to have the inspector check your work.

Estimating & Ordering Materials

Use this chart to help you estimate the materials you will need for landscaping projects. Sizes and weights of materials may vary, so consult your supplier for more detailed information on estimating materials.

If you are unfamiliar with the gravel and stone products available in your area, visit a sand-and-gravel supplier to see the products first-hand.

When sand, gravel, and other bulk materials are delivered, place them on a tarp to protect your yard. Make sure the tarp is as close to the work area as possible.

Methods for Estimating Materials	
Sand, gravel, topsoil (2" layer)	surface area (sq. ft.) ÷ 100 = tons needed
Standard brick pavers (4" × 8")	surface area (sq. ft.) × 5 = number of pavers needed
Poured concrete (4" layer)	surface area (sq. ft.) × .012 = cubic yards needed
Flagstone	surface area (sq. ft.) ÷ 100 = tons of stone needed
Interlocking block (6" × 16" face)	area of wall face (sq. ft.) × 1.5 = number of stones needed
Retaining wall timbers (5" × 6" × 8 ft.)	area of wall face (sq. ft.) ÷ 3 = number of timbers needed
Cut stone for 1-ft.-thick walls	area of wall face (sq. ft.) ÷ 15 = tons of stone needed
Rubble stone for 1-ft.-thick walls	area of wall face (sq. ft.) ÷ 35 = tons of stone needed
8 × 8 × 16 concrete block for free-standing walls	height of wall (ft.) × length of wall × 1.125 = number of blocks

Using Landscape Professionals

Using landscape professionals can save work time and simplify large, complicated projects. Professional designers can help you plan and budget your project, and contractors can save you work time on large, difficult tasks.

The abilities and reputations of designers and contractors vary greatly, so always check references and insist on viewing samples of previous work before hiring a professional. Make sure to get a written, itemized estimate; terms for payment; and proof of bonding and insurance.

Landscape Professionals

Landscape architect: a licensed structural designer who is qualified to plan large, highly technical structures, like a tall retaining wall or free-standing garden wall, an in-ground swimming pool, or gazebo.

Landscape designer: a general-purpose design professional, often affiliated with a large nursery. Reputable landscape designers are the best choice for designing and planning help.

Garden designer: usually employed at a garden center or nursery. Garden designers can help you choose plants and plan gardening areas.

Landscape contractor: supplies workers and supervises labor for a wide range of landscaping projects. Landscaping contractors range from small one- and two-man crews to large, well-established companies that can oversee all stages of a landscape project.

Excavating contractor: provides labor and machinery required for large digging and excavation projects. Make sure utility companies locate and mark underground lines before the contractor begins work.

Concrete contractor: a specialized professional skilled at pouring and finishing concrete patios, driveways, sidewalks, steps, and walls.

Common supplies for landscape construction include: (A) sheet plastic, (B) landscape fabric, (C) burlap, (D) stucco lath, (E) bendable rigid plastic edging, (F) post caps, (G) wood sealer-preservative, (H) mason's string, (I) rigid plastic edging, (J) flexible plastic edging, (K) rope, (L) perforated drain pipe, (M) masonry sealer, (N) splash block for runoff water.

Landscaping Supplies

In addition to the visible design materials used in a landscape, there are many hidden, structural supplies that are equally important to successful landscaping projects.

Because landscape structures are exposed to weather extremes, make sure to invest in the best materials you can afford. Buying cheap materials to save a few dollars can shorten the life span of a landscape structure by many years.

Metal connecting materials, including nails, screws, fence hardware, and post anchors should be made from aluminum or galvanized steel, which will not rust.

Check grade stamps on pressure-treated lumber. Look for lumber treated with chromated copper arsenate, identified by the "CCA" label printed on the grade stamp. For above-ground and ground-contact applications, choose lumber graded "LP-22" or ".40 retention." If wood will be buried, use lumber graded "FDN" or ".60 retention," if it is available.

Base materials for landscape walls and paved surfaces include: (A) sand, (B) seed gravel, (C) compactible gravel subbase containing a large amount of clay and lime, (D) topsoil, (E) coarse gravel, used as backfill, (F) mortar mix, and (G) concrete mix.

Connecting materials for landscape construction include: (A) galvanized common nails, (B) galvanized finish nails, (C) self-tapping masonry anchors, (D) galvanized utility screws, (E) 12" galvanized spikes, (F) concrete reinforcement bars, (G) lead masonry anchors, (H) metal pipes for anchoring timbers, (I) lag screws with washers, (J) construction adhesive, (K) J-bolts, (L) galvanized post anchor, (M) rafter strap, (N) fence bracket.

Basic yard and garden tools used in landscape construction and maintenance include: (A) garden shovel, (B) hand shears, (C) pruning shears, (D) garden rake, (E) spade, (F) power trimmer, (G) hoe, (H) garden hose, (I) bow saw, (J) line-feed trimmer, (K) pressure sprayer.

Tools for Landscape Construction

Most landscape construction projects can be done with ordinary garden tools and workshop tools you already own. If you need to buy new tools, always invest in high-quality products. A few specialty tools, most of which can be borrowed or rented, make some jobs easier.

When using power tools outdoors, always use a GFCI (ground-fault circuit-interrupter) extension cord for safety. After each use, clean and dry metal tools to prevent rust.

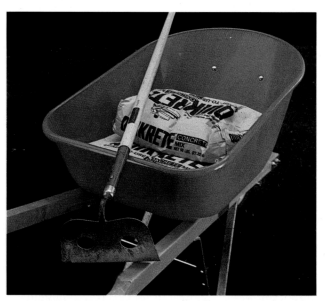

A sturdy wheelbarrow is an essential tool for landscape construction and maintenance. Better wheelbarrows have inflatable rubber tires and wooden handles.

Basic hand and power tools used in landscape construction include: (A) reciprocating saw, (B) hammer, (C) hand maul, (D) rubber mallet, (E) pencil, (F) circular saw, (G) eye protection, (H) drill with bits, (I) line level, (J) carpenter's level, (K) carpenter's square, (L) plumb bob and chalk line, (M) tape measures, (N) GFCI extension cord, (O) particle mask, (P) work gloves, (Q) caulk gun, (R) hearing protectors.

Specialty tools you can rent include: (A) tamping machine, (B) "jumping jack" tamping machine, (C) sod cutter, (D) power auger, (E) hand tamper, (F) chain saw.

Tools for masonry work include: (A) mortar bag, (B) masonry chisel, (C) V-shaped mortar tool, (D) stiff broom, (E) masonry drill bits, (F) concrete float, (G) pointed trowel, (H) standard trowel, (I) rubber gloves, (J) masonry saw blade.

Build contours to create visual interest in a flat landscape. Contours should have gentle slopes and irregular shapes that accent the surrounding yard. Contours can be used to create a visual barrier, or to provide planting areas (pages 76 to 77).

Hire an excavating contractor if you need to move large amounts of soil. Small front-end loaders are available for daily rental, but using them successfully requires some practice.

Grading & Contouring Your Yard

Reshaping, removing, or adding soil is an important step in many landscaping projects. If you are installing a patio, for example, you may need to first create a large area that is very flat. Or you may want to put a finishing touch on a landscape by adding raised contours or planting areas to the yard.

Consider how the overall slope affects drainage in your yard. Make sure your finished landscape is graded so it directs runoff water away from buildings and minimizes low-lying areas that can trap standing water. To identify drainage problems, examine your yard immediately after a heavy rain, or after watering it thoroughly, and look for areas where water collects or flows toward building foundations.

Before digging, contact utility companies to pinpoint and mark the location of underground wires or pipes. You can arrange to have utility lines rerouted if there is no way to work around them.

Everything You Need:

Tools: hose, shovel, tape measure, garden rake, wheelbarrow, hammer or maul, line level.

Materials (as needed): edging material, topsoil, gravel, string, stakes, perforated drain pipe, splash block, sod, landscape fabric.

How to Create a Landscape Contour

1 Create an outline of the planned contour on your lawn, using a hose or rope. If the contour will be used as a planting area, install edging material along the outline.

2 Fill the outlined area with topsoil. Use a rake to shape the soil into a smooth mound no more than 18" high, then tamp and water the soil to compress it. Landscape contours can be finished with sod or used as planting areas (pages 76 to 77).

How to Grade Soil Around Foundations

Prevent water damage to foundations by grading soil so there is a smooth, gradual slope away from the building. For proper drainage, the ground within 6 ft. of a foundation should drop 3/4" for each foot of distance. To check the grade, attach a string to a pair of stakes and adjust the string so it is level. Measure down from the string at 1-ft. intervals to determine the grade. If necessary, add extra soil and shape it with a garden rake to get the proper grade.

Tips for Solving Drainage Problems

Fill small low-lying areas by top-dressing them with black soil. Spread the new soil into an even layer, then compress it with a hand tamper.

Improve drainage in a large low-lying area by creating a shallow ditch, called a drainage swale, to carry runoff water away. If your region receives frequent heavy rainfalls, or if you have dense soil that drains poorly, you may need to lay a perforated drain pipe and a bed of gravel under the swale to make it more effective (page opposite).

How to Make a Drainage Swale

1 After identifying the problem area, use stakes to mark a swale route that will direct water away from the site toward a runoff area. The outlet of the swale must be lower than any point in the problem area.

2 Dig a 6"-deep, rounded trench along the swale route. If you remove the sod carefully, you can lay it back into the trench when the swale is completed.

3 Shape the trench so it slopes gradually downward toward the outlet, and the sides and bottom are smooth.

4 Complete the swale by laying sod into the trench. Compress the sod, then water the area thoroughly to check the drainage.

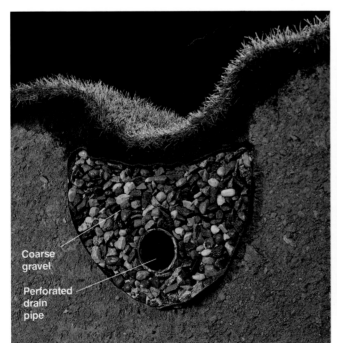

Coarse gravel

Perforated drain pipe

Splash block

OPTION: For severe drainage problems, dig a 1-ft.-deep swale angled slightly downward to the outlet point. Line the swale with landscape fabric. Spread a 2" layer of coarse gravel in the bottom of the swale, then lay perforated drain pipe over the gravel. Cover the pipe with a 5" layer of gravel, then wrap the landscape fabric over the top of the gravel. Cover the swale with soil and fresh sod. Set a splash block at the outlet to distribute the runoff and prevent erosion.

Cut stone is a top-quality, expensive building material used for retaining walls (shown above) and free-standing garden walls. For retaining walls, cut stone is laid without mortar to improve drainage, except for the top row, which can be anchored with mortar for extra strength. Retaining wall designs often include garden steps. For free-standing garden walls, cut stones usually are mortared. When built correctly, cut-stone walls can last for generations. See pages 24 to 25.

Landscape Walls

Landscape walls include retaining walls and free-standing walls. They can define outdoor areas, increase the amount of level yard area, stop soil erosion, and improve the appearance of your yard and home.

Many stone, concrete, and wood products can be used to build landscape walls. When choosing materials, consider style, cost, ease of installation, and durability.

Wherever possible, limit the height of your landscape walls to 3 ft. Local Building Codes usually require deep concrete footings and special construction techniques for taller landscape walls.

Retaining walls are subject to enormous pressure from the weight of the soil behind the wall. To offset this pressure, build the retaining wall so each row of materials is set slightly behind the previous row. The backward angle of a retaining wall (at least 1" for every foot in height) is called the "batter." For maximum strength, some landscape contractors tilt the entire wall back into the hillside.

Common Materials Used for Landscape Walls

Landscape timbers are inexpensive and easy to cut at any angle, but are less durable than stone or masonry. A well-built timber retaining wall made with good-quality pressure-treated lumber will last for 15 to 20 years in most climates. See pages 22 to 23.

Rubble stone is used for both retaining walls and free-standing garden walls, and usually is laid without mortar. Building rubble-stone walls requires patience, but the materials are less expensive than cut stone or interlocking block. See page 24.

Interlocking block made from cast concrete is the easiest of all materials to work with. It makes very strong and durable retaining walls, and is less expensive than cut stone. Interlocking block is especially useful for curved retaining walls. See pages 19 to 21.

Concrete block is inexpensive and is available in decorative and plain styles. Concrete block requires mortar, and makes a very sturdy free-standing garden wall. But because the mortared joints hinder drainage, concrete block is a poor choice for retaining walls. See pages 26 to 31.

Terraced retaining walls work well on steep hillsides. Two or more short retaining walls are easier to install and more stable than a single, tall retaining wall. Construct the terraces so each wall is no higher than 3 ft.

Building a Retaining Wall

The main reason to build retaining walls is to create level planting areas or prevent erosion on hillsides. But if you have a flat yard, you also can build low retaining wall structures to make decorative raised planting beds and add visual interest to the landscape.

No matter what material is used, a retaining wall can be damaged if water saturates the soil behind it. To ensure its durability, make sure your wall contains the proper drainage features (page opposite).

Retaining walls taller than 3 ft. are subject to thousands of pounds of pressure from the weight of the soil and water, so they require special building techniques that are best left to a professional. If you have a tall hillside, it is best to terrace the hill with several short walls (photo, above).

Before excavating for a retaining wall, **check with local utility companies** to make sure there are no underground pipes or cables running through the site.

Everything You Need for Retaining Walls

Tools: wheelbarrow, shovel, garden rake, line level, hand tamper, rented tamping machine, small maul, masonry chisel, eye protection, hearing protectors, work gloves, circular saw, level, tape measure, marking pencil.

Materials: stakes, mason's string, landscape fabric, compactible gravel subbase, perforated drain pipe, coarse backfill gravel.

Added supplies for interlocking block walls: masonry blade for circular saw, caulk gun, construction adhesive.

Added supplies for stone walls: masonry chisel, masonry blade for circular saw, trowel, mortar mix.

Added supplies for timber walls: chain saw or reciprocating saw, drill and 1" spade bit, 12" galvanized spikes.

Options for Positioning a Retaining Wall

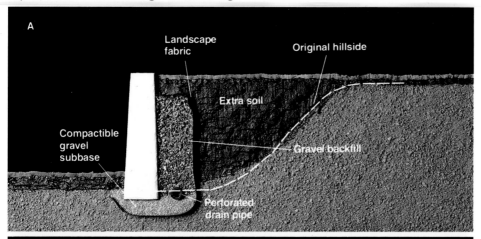

(A) Increase the level area above the wall by positioning the wall well forward from the top of the hill. Fill in behind the wall with extra soil, available from sand-and-gravel companies.

(B) Keep the basic shape of your yard by positioning the wall near the top of the hillside. Use the soil removed at the base of the hill to fill in near the top of the wall.

Structural features for all retaining walls include: a compactible gravel subbase to make a solid footing for the wall, coarse gravel backfill and a perforated drain pipe to improve drainage behind the wall, and landscape fabric to keep the loose soil from washing into the gravel backfill.

Providing Drainage for Retaining Walls

Backfill with gravel and install a perforated drain pipe near the bottom of the gravel backfill. Vent the pipe to the side or bottom of the retaining wall, where runoff water can flow away from the hillside without causing erosion.

Dig a swale, a shallow ditch 1 ft. to 2 ft. away from the top of the wall, to direct runoff water away from the retaining wall (see pages 12 to 13). This technique is useful for sites that have very dense soil that does not drain well.

How to Prepare a Retaining Wall Site

1 Excavate the hillside, if necessary, to create a level base for the retaining wall. For interlocking blocks or stone walls, allow at least 12" of space for gravel backfill between the back of the wall and the hillside. For timber walls, allow at least 3 ft. of space. When excavating large areas, rent earth-moving equipment or hire a contractor.

2 Use stakes to mark the front edge of the wall at the ends and at any corners and curves. Connect the stakes with mason's string. Use a line level to check the string, and, if necessary, adjust the string so it is level.

3 Dig a trench for the first row of building materials, measuring down from the mason's string to maintain a level trench. Make the trench 6" deeper than the thickness of one layer of building material. For example, if you are using 6"-thick interlocking blocks, make the trench 12" deep.

4 Line the excavation with strips of landscape fabric cut 3 ft. longer than the planned height of the wall. Make sure seams overlap by at least 6".

Building a Retaining Wall Using Interlocking Block

Several styles of interlocking block are available at building and outdoor centers. Most types have a natural rock finish that combines the rough texture of cut stone with the uniform shape and size of concrete blocks.

Interlocking blocks weigh up to 80 lbs. each, so it is a good idea to have helpers when building a retaining wall. Suppliers offer substantial discounts when interlocking block is purchased in large quantities, so you may be able to save money if you coordinate your own project with those of your neighbors.

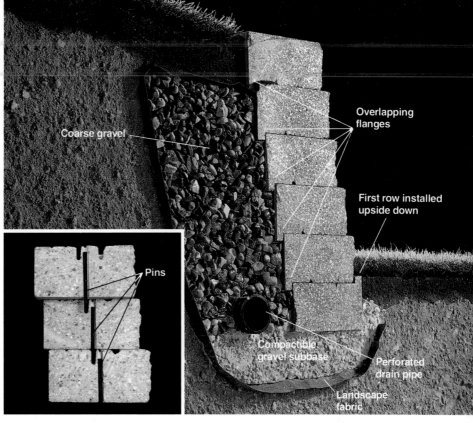

Interlocking wall blocks do not need mortar. Some types are held together with a system of overlapping flanges that automatically set the backward angle (batter) as the blocks are stacked. Other types of blocks use a pinning system (inset).

Tips for Building a Retaining Wall Using Interlocking Block

Make a stepped trench when the ends of a retaining wall must blend into an existing hillside. Retaining walls often are designed so the ends curve or turn back into the slope.

Make half-blocks by scoring full blocks with a circular saw and masonry blade, then breaking the blocks along the scored line with a maul and chisel. Half-blocks are used when making corners, and to ensure that vertical joints between blocks are staggered between rows.

19

1 Spread a 6" layer of compactible gravel subbase into the trench and pack thoroughly. A rented tamping machine, sometimes called a "jumping jack," works better than a hand tamper (step 7) for packing the subbase.

2 Lay the first row of blocks into the trench, aligning the front edges with the mason's string. When using flanged blocks, place the first row of blocks upside down and backward. Check the blocks frequently with a level, and adjust, if necessary, by adding or removing subbase material below the blocks.

3 Lay the second row of blocks according to manufacturer's instructions. On flanged blocks, the blocks should be laid so the flanges are tight against the underlying blocks. Check regularly to make sure the blocks are level.

4 Add 6" of gravel behind the blocks, making sure the landscape fabric remains between the gravel and the hillside. Pack the gravel thoroughly with a hand tamper.

5 Place perforated drain pipe on top of the gravel, at least 6" behind wall, with perforations facing down. Make sure that at least one end of the pipe is unobstructed so runoff water can escape (page 17). Lay additional rows of blocks until the wall is about 18" above ground level. Make sure the vertical joints in adjoining rows are offset.

6 Fill behind the wall with coarse gravel, and pack well. Lay the remaining rows of block, except for the cap row, backfilling with gravel and packing with a hand tamper as you go.

7 Before laying the cap blocks, fold the end of the landscape fabric over the gravel backfill. Add a thin layer of topsoil over the fabric, then pack it thoroughly with a hand tamper.

8 Fold any excess landscape fabric back over the soil, then apply construction adhesive to the blocks. Lay the cap blocks in place. Use topsoil to fill in behind the wall and to fill in the trench at the base of the wall. Install sod or other plants, as desired.

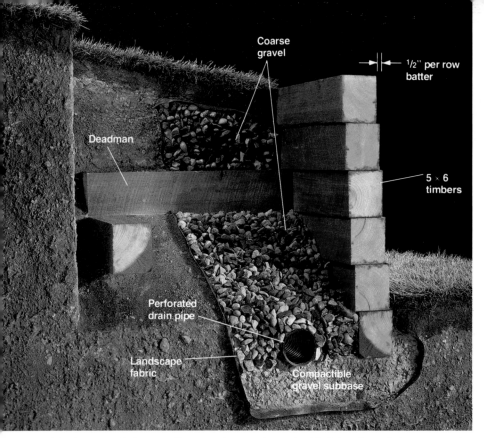

Coarse gravel

Deadman

1/2" per row batter

5 × 6 timbers

Perforated drain pipe

Landscape fabric

Compactible gravel subbase

Building a Retaining Wall Using Timbers

Timber walls have a life span of 15 to 20 years if built correctly. Use pressure-treated timbers at least 5 × 6 in size. Smaller timbers are not sturdy enough for retaining walls.

Use a chain saw or a reciprocating saw to cut landscape timbers. The pesticides used in treated lumber are toxic, so wear a particle mask, gloves, and long sleeves when cutting or handling pressure-treated lumber. Avoid using old timbers, like discarded railroad ties, that have been soaked in creosote. Creosote can leach into the soil and kill plants.

Before building the retaining wall, prepare the site as directed on page 18.

Timber retaining walls must be anchored with "deadmen" that extend from the wall back into the soil. Deadmen prevent the wall from sagging under the weight of the soil. For best results with timber retaining walls, create a backward angle (batter) by setting each row of timbers 1/2" behind the preceding row. The first row of timbers should be buried.

Tips for Strengthening a Timber Retaining Wall

Timber depth equal to 1/2 exposed height

Use metal reinforcement bars instead of spikes for extra strength when connecting timbers. Cut 12" to 24" lengths of bar with sharp points, then drive them into pilot holes drilled through the top timber, spaced at 2-ft. intervals. This technique is especially useful if you have heavy, dense soil that drains poorly.

Install vertical anchor posts to reinforce the wall. Space the posts 3 ft. apart, and install them so the buried depth of each post is at least half the exposed height of the wall. Anchor posts are essential if it is not practical to install deadmen (photo, top).

How to Build a Retaining Wall Using Timbers

1 Spread a 6" layer of compactible gravel subbase into the prepared trench, then tamp the subbase and begin laying timbers, following the same techniques as with interlocking blocks (steps 1 to 7, pages 20 to 21). Each row of timbers should be set with a 1/2" batter, and end joints should be staggered so they do not align.

2 Use 12" galvanized spikes or reinforcement bars to anchor the ends of each timber to the underlying timbers. Stagger the ends of the timbers to form strong corner joints. Drive additional spikes along the length of the timbers at 2-ft. intervals. If you have trouble driving the spikes, drill pilot holes.

3 Install deadmen, spaced 4 ft. apart, midway up the wall. Build the deadmen by joining 3-ft.-long lengths of timber with 12" spikes, then insert the ends through holes cut in the landscape fabric. Anchor deadmen to wall with spikes. Install the remaining rows of timbers, and finish backfilling behind the wall (steps 6 to 8, page 21).

4 Improve drainage by drilling weep holes through the second row of landscape timbers and into the gravel backfill, using a spade bit. Space the holes 4 ft. apart, and angle them upward.

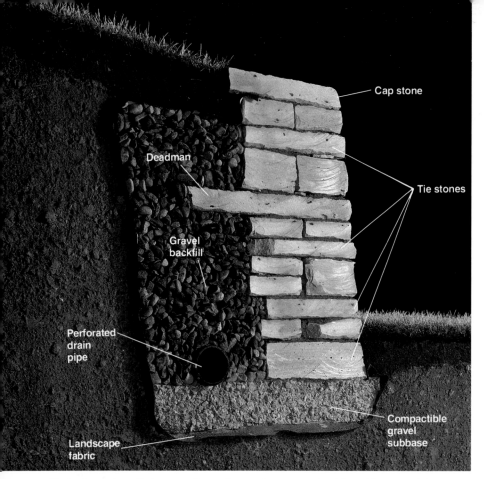

Building a Retaining Wall Using Natural Stone

Retaining walls made from natural cut stone or rubble stone give a traditional, timeless look to a landscape. Natural stone walls usually are laid without mortar, although the last one or two rows can be mortared in place for greater strength. Unlike mortared stone or block walls (pages 26 to 31), unmortared stone walls require no concrete footings.

Before building the remaining wall, prepare the site as directed on page 18. Build the wall by placing the largest stones at the bottom and reserving the smoothest, flattest stones for the corners and the top (cap) row.

Cut stone has flat, smooth surfaces for easy stacking. For a stable retaining wall, alternate rows of "tie stones" that span the entire width of the wall with rows of smaller stones. Install extra-long stones (called deadmen) that extend back into gravel backfill, spaced every 4 to 6 ft.

Retaining Wall Variations Using Rubble Stone

Boulders are large, uncut rocks, usually round in shape. The retaining wall site requires no subbase or backfill: simply dig out the hillside to fit the shape of the boulders and roll them into place. Boulders range in size from about 40 lbs. to several hundred lbs. For heavy boulders, you may want to hire a contractor to deliver and position the rocks.

Field stone refers to any irregular assortment of rough rock. You can gather field stone by hand or buy it from sand-and-gravel companies. Field-stone retaining walls do not need a subbase or backfill; but for better stability, build the wall so it tilts back into the hillside. Pack the open spaces between rocks with rock fragments or soil. If you wish, plant vines or groundcover in the exposed gaps.

How to Build a Retaining Wall Using Cut Stone

1 Spread a 6" layer of compactible gravel subbase into the prepared trench (step 1, page 20), then sort the stones by size and shape so they can be located easily as you build. Make sure you have enough long stones to serve as tie stones, deadmen, and cap stones.

2 Trim irregular stones, if needed, to make them fit solidly into the wall. Always wear eye protection and hearing protectors when cutting stone. Score the stone first using a masonry blade and circular saw set to $1/8$" blade depth, then drive a masonry chisel along the scored line until the stone breaks.

3 Lay rows of stones, following the same techniques for backfilling as for interlocking blocks (steps 2 to 7, pages 20 to 21). Build a backward slant (batter) into the wall by setting each row of stones about $1/2$" back from the preceding row. For stability, work tie stones and deadmen into the wall at frequent intervals.

4 Before laying the cap row of stones, mix mortar according to manufacturer's directions and apply a thick bed along the tops of the installed stones, keeping the mortar at least 6" from the front face of the wall. Lay the cap stones, and press them into the mortar. Because the mortar is not visible, this technique is called "blind mortaring." Finish backfilling behind the wall (step 8, page 21).

A stucco finish and lattice panels turn a plain concrete block wall into a durable, attractive privacy wall. See pages 32 to 33 for these finishing techniques.

Other Options for Finishing a Concrete Block Wall

Stone veneer (sometimes called cultured stone) copies the look of natural stone at a fraction of the cost. Available in dozens of different styles, stone veneer kits come with an assortment of flat pieces and corner pieces. The veneer is held in place with a layer of standard mortar (page 33).

Decorative block adds visual interest to a plain concrete block wall. Check with your local building inspector before adding block to a wall, since the added height may require extra reinforcement. Decorative block also may be used to build an entire wall (page 15).

Building a Free-standing Wall

A free-standing wall serves the same function as a hedge or fence, but is much sturdier. Walls are popular in areas where growing shrubs and hedges is difficult. Free-standing walls can train climbing plants or support trellises or container plants. Low walls may be used as garden benches.

Most free-standing walls are built by mortaring concrete block, brick, or natural stone. The following pages show how to build a concrete block wall, but similar techniques can be used for any mortared wall.

Free-standing walls also can be built from unmortared stones, using techniques similar to those used in building a stone retaining wall (pages 24 to 25).

Limit your walls to 3 ft. in height. Taller walls need deep footings and extra reinforcement. Increase privacy by adding a trellis to the wall (photo, top left). Many local Building Codes limit the total height of the wall and trellis to 6 ft.

Everything You Need:

Tools: tape measure, rake, hammer, level, shovel, wheelbarrow, old paint brush, chalk line, trowel, rubber gloves, pencil, line level, masonry chisel, masonry hammer, V-shaped mortar tool, garden hoe, level.

Materials: rope, stakes, 2 × 6 lumber, compactible gravel subbase, reinforcement rods, oil, premixed concrete, concrete blocks, sheet plastic, 3/8"-thick wood strips, mortar mix, mason's string.

How to Install a Footing for a Free-standing Wall

1 Lay out the rough position of the wall, using a rope.

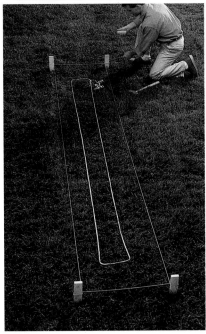

2 Outline the wall footing, using stakes and mason's string. Check the string with a line level and adjust as needed. The footing should be twice as wide as the planned wall, and should extend 1 ft. beyond each end.

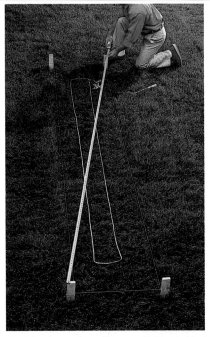

3 Measure the diagonals to make sure the outline is square, and adjust as necessary. Dig a 1-ft.-deep trench for the footing, using the strings as a guide. Make sure the bottom of the trench is roughly level.

4 Lay a 6" layer of compactible gravel subbase into the trench. Tamp the subbase thoroughly (page 21). NOTE: Follow local Building Code guidelines for footing depth.

5 Build a wood form using 2 × 6 lumber, and set it in the trench. Add or remove subbase material to level the form. Drive stakes along the outside of the form to anchor it.

6 Lay reinforcement bars inside the form to make the footing more crack-resistant. Set the bars on 2 × 4 scraps, a few inches inside the form. Coat the inside of the form with oil for easy removal.

(continued next page)

How to Install a Footing for a Free-standing Wall (continued)

7 Fill the form up to the top of the boards with concrete. Work the concrete with a shovel just enough to remove air pockets.

8 Smooth off (screed) the surface of the concrete by dragging a short 2 × 4 along the top of the form. Add concrete to any low areas, and screed again.

9 When concrete is hard to the touch, cover it with plastic and let it cure for 2 or 3 days. When surface has cured, pry the forms loose with a shovel.

How to Build a Free-standing Wall Using Concrete Block

1 Test-fit a row of blocks on the footing, using smooth-sided end blocks at the ends. You may need to use half-blocks on one end to achieve the desired wall length. Use 3/8"-thick wood strips or dowels as spacers to maintain an even gap for mortar between the blocks.

Reference lines

2 Draw pencil lines on the concrete to mark the ends of the test-fitted row. Extend the line well past the edges of the block. Use a chalk line to snap reference lines on each side of the footing, 3" from the blocks. These reference lines will serve as a guide when setting the blocks into mortar.

Wider flanges

3 Remove the blocks and set them nearby. Mix mortar in a wheelbarrow or large pail, following manufacturer's directions. Mortar should be moist enough to hold its shape when squeezed.

4 Trowel thick lines of mortar, slightly wider and longer than the base of the end block, onto the center of the footing. If the footing has cured for over a week, dampen it before mortaring.

TIP: When positioning concrete blocks, make sure the side with the wider flanges is facing upward. The wider flanges provide more surface for applying mortar.

5 Set an end block into the mortar, so the end is aligned with the pencil mark on the footing. Set a level on top of the block, then tap the block with a trowel handle until it is level. Use the chalkline as a reference point for keeping the block in line.

6 Apply mortar, then set and level the block at the opposite end of the footing. Stake a mason's string even with the top outside corners of the blocks. Check the string with a line level, then adjust the blocks to align with the string. Remove excess mortar, and fill the gaps beneath the end blocks (inset).

(continued next page)

7 Apply mortar to the vertical flanges on one side of a standard block (inset) and to the footing, using a trowel. Set the block next to the end block, leaving a 3/8" layer of mortar between blocks. Tap the block into position with a trowel handle, using the string as a guide to align the block.

8 Install the remaining blocks, working back and forth from opposite ends. Be careful to maintain 3/8" joints to ensure that the last block in the row will fit. Make sure the row is level and straight by aligning the blocks with the mason's string and checking them with a carpenter's level.

9 At the middle of the row, apply mortar to the vertical flanges on both sides of the last block, then slide the block down into place. Align the last block with the mason's string.

10 Apply a 1" layer of mortar to the top flanges of the end blocks. Scrape off any mortar that falls onto the footing.

11 Begin laying the second row. Use half-size end blocks to create staggered vertical joints. Check with a straightedge to make sure the new blocks are aligned with the bottom blocks.

VARIATION: If your wall has a corner, begin the second row with a full-sized end block that spans the vertical joint formed where two sides of the wall meet. This creates staggered vertical joints.

12 Insert a nail into the wet mortar at each end of the wall. Attach a mason's string to one nail, then stretch the string up over the corners of the end blocks and tie it to the nail at the opposite end.

13 Install the second row of blocks, using the same method as with the first row. When the second row is completed, remove the nails and mason's string. Scrape off excess mortar, and finish the joints with a V-shaped mortar tool. Install each additional row of blocks by repeating steps 11 to 13. Finish the joints as each row of blocks is completed.

14 Complete the wall with a row of cap blocks. Cap blocks are very heavy, and must be laid gently to keep mortar from being squeezed out. If you are adding lattice panels to the top of the wall, insert J-bolts into the joints between the cap blocks while mortar is still wet (page 32).

How to Add Lattice Panels to a Block Wall

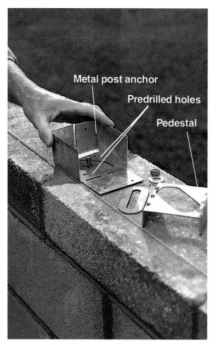

1 While mortar is still wet, install ³/₈"-diameter J-bolts into the center of the cap row joints at post locations. About 1" of the bolt should protrude. Pack mortar around the bolt and let it harden. (If mortar already has hardened, see OPTION, step 2.)

2 Align and attach a metal post anchor at each post location. Slip an oval washer over each J-bolt, then attach a nut. OPTION: Attach metal post anchors by driving self-tapping masonry anchors through the predrilled holes in the bottom of the post anchor.

3 Set a metal pedestal into each anchor. The top of the J-bolt should be below the pedestal.

4 Cut a 4 × 4 post for each anchor. Set the post on the pedestal, then bend the open flange up against the post. Make sure the post is plumb, then attach it with 6d galvanized nails.

5 Center and install fence brackets on the posts, and slide the framed lattice panels into the brackets from above until the panels rest on the bottom flanges of the lowest brackets. Most lattice panels are 8 ft. long, and can be cut to fit if your posts are spaced less than 8 ft. apart.

How to Finish a Block Wall with Stucco

1 Attach wire lath to the entire surface of all wall faces, using self-tapping masonry anchors. Lath provides a surface for application of stucco or mortar (step 1, below).

2 Mix stucco, using a ratio of 3 parts sand and 2 parts portland cement, adding enough water so the mixture holds its shape when squeezed. Trowel a 3/8"-thick layer directly onto the metal lath. Scratch grooves into the surface of the stucco, then let the coat cure for two days. Dampen a few times daily.

3 Apply a second 3/8" layer of the same stucco mixture over the first coat. Do not scratch this layer. Let stucco cure for two days. Dampen a few times daily.

4 Mix a finish stucco coat, using 1 part lime, 3 parts sand, and 6 parts white cement. Dampen walls, and dab a finish coat onto the wall, using a whisk broom.

5 Flatten the surface of the finish coat with a trowel. Dampen the wall daily for three or four days to complete the curing.

How to Apply Stone Veneer to a Block Wall

1 Prepare wall with wire lath (step 1, above), then apply a 1/2"-thick layer of standard mortar to the wall. Scratch grooves into the damp mortar, using the trowel tip, then allow to dry overnight. Beginning at the bottom of the wall, apply mortar to the back of each veneer piece, then press it onto the wall with a twisting motion. Keep a 1/2" gap between pieces.

2 After mortar has dried for a day, fill the joints with fresh mortar, using a mortar bag. Use a V-shaped mortar tool to finish the joints (step 13, page 31).

Flagstone walkways combine charm with durability, and work well in both casual and formal settings. Also a popular material for patios, flagstone can be set in sand, or it can be mortared in place. See pages 38 to 39. TIP: Prevent damage to the edging material by trimming near the walkway with a line-feed trimmer instead of a mower.

Building Walkways & Paths

Walkways and paths serve as "hallways" between heavily used areas of your yard, and can be used to direct traffic toward a favorite landscape feature, like a pond. Walkways also create a visual corridor that directs the eye from one area to another.

Curved paths give a softer, more relaxed look to a landscape, but straight or angular paths and walkways fit well in contemporary landscape designs.

Garden paths often are made from loose materials, like crushed rock or bark, held in place by edging. Walkways are more durable when made from stone or brick paving materials set in sand or mortar. Poured concrete sidewalks are practical and the most durable, but unless you have a lot of experience pouring and curing concrete, do not attempt to build them yourself. Most paving techniques used in patio construction (pages 50 to 59) can be used for walkways as well.

Everything You Need:

Tools: tape measure, spade, garden rake, rubber mallet, circular saw with masonry blade, masonry chisel, masonry hammer.

Materials: landscape fabric, garden hose, edging material (page 36), walkway surface materials, galvanized screws, 2 × 6 lumber. Added supplies for mortared brick walkways: mortar, mortar bag, V-shaped mortar tool, trowel.

Loose materials, such as gravel, crushed rock, wood chips and bark, make informal, inexpensive pathways that are well suited for light-traffic areas. Build loose-material paths with the surface material slightly above ground level, to keep it from being washed away.

Brick pavers provide stately charm to a main walkway, making a house more appealing from the street. Because pavers are very durable, they are ideal for heavy-traffic areas. Brick pavers can be set in sand, or mortared in place over an old concrete surface. Pavers used for mortared walkways often are thinner than those designed for sand installation.

Tips for Building a Walkway

Use a sod cutter to strip grass from your pathway site. Available at most rental centers, sod cutters excavate to a very even depth. The cut sod can be replanted in other parts of your lawn.

Install stakes and strings when laying out straight walkways made from stone paving materials, and measure from the strings to ensure straight sides and uniform excavation depth.

Loose material
Landscape fabric
Brick edging

Brick edging makes a good boundary for both straight and curved paths made from loose materials. See page 37.

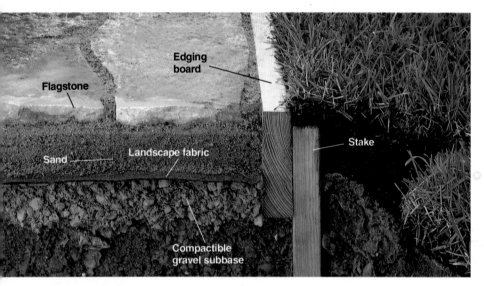

Edging board
Flagstone
Stake
Sand
Landscape fabric
Compactible gravel subbase

Wood edging makes a sturdy border for straight walkways made from flagstone or brick pavers set in sand. See pages 38 to 39.

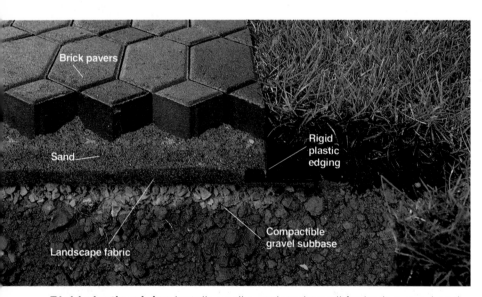

Brick pavers
Rigid plastic edging
Sand
Landscape fabric
Compactible gravel subbase

Rigid plastic edging installs easily, and works well for both curved and straight walkways made from paving stones or brick pavers set in sand. See pages 50 to 59.

Types of Edging

Use edging to keep walkway materials in place. Consider cost, appearance, flexibility, and ease of installation when selecting an edging type.

Brick edging set in soil is good for casual, lightly traveled pathways, but should be used only in soil that is dense and well drained. (Bricks in loose or swampy soil will not hold their position.) Bricks can be set vertically, or tilted at an angle to make a saw-tooth pattern. Brick pavers also can be mortared to the sides of an old sidewalk to create a border for a new surface (pages 40 to 41).

Wood edging made from pressure-treated lumber, redwood, or cedar is inexpensive and easy to install. The tops of the boards are left exposed to create an attractive border. The wood edging boards are held in place by attaching them to recessed wood stakes spaced every 12" along the outside of the edging.

Rigid plastic edging is inconspicuous, durable, and easy to install. It was developed as an edging for brick pavers set in sand. Rigid plastic edging is held in place by the weight of the soil and with galvanized spikes driven through the back flange. Rolled vinyl edging is used most often to make boundaries for planting areas (pages 76 to 77), but also works as an edging for casual walkways. It is inexpensive and very flexible.

How to Build a Path Using Loose Materials & Brick Edging

1 Outline the path using a garden hose or rope, then excavate the site to a depth of 2" to 3" using a spade, hoe, or a rented sod cutter (page 35). Rake the site smooth.

2 Dig narrow edging trenches about 2" deeper than the path site along both edges of the excavation, using a spade or hoe.

3 Lay landscaping fabric between the edging trenches to prevent weeds from growing. Overlap sheets by at least 6".

4 Set bricks on end into the edging trenches, with the tops slightly above ground level. Pack soil behind and beneath each brick, adjusting the bricks, if necessary, to keep the rows even.

5 Finish the path by spreading loose material (gravel, crushed rock, bark, or wood chips) between the rows of edging bricks. Level the surface with a garden rake. The loose material should be slightly above ground level. Tap each brick lightly on the inside face to help set it into the soil. Inspect and adjust the bricks yearly, adding new loose material as needed.

How to Build a Flagstone Walkway Using Wood Edging

1 Outline the walkway site and excavate to a depth of 6". Allow enough room for the edging and stakes (step 2). For straight walkways, use stakes and strings to maintain a uniform outline (page 35). Add a 2" layer of compactible gravel subbase, using a rake to smooth the surface.

2 Install 2 × 6 edging made from pressure-treated lumber around the sides of the site. Drive 12" stakes on the outside of the edging, spaced 12" apart. Tops of the stakes should be below ground level. Attach the edging to the stakes using galvanized screws.

3 Test-fit the flagstones to find an efficient, attractive arrangement of stones. Arrange the stones to minimize the number of cuts needed. Leave a gap between stones that is at least 3/8", but no more than 2" wide. Use a pencil to mark stones for cutting, then remove the stones and set them nearby.

4 Cut flagstones by scoring along the marked lines with a circular saw and masonry blade set to 1/8" blade depth. Set a piece of wood under the stone, just inside the scored line, then use a masonry chisel and hammer to strike along the scored line until the stone breaks.

5 Lay sheets of landscape fabric over the walkway site to prevent plants and grass from growing up between the stones. (Omit the landscape fabric if you want to plant grass or ground cover to fill the cracks.) Spread a 2" layer of sand over the landscape fabric to serve as the base for the flagstones.

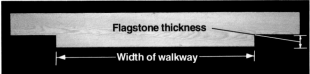

Flagstone thickness

Width of walkway

6 Make a "screed" for smoothing the sand by notching the ends of a short 2 × 6 to fit inside the edging (see inset). The depth of the notches should equal the thickness of the stones, usually about 2". Screed the base by pulling the 2 × 6 from one end of the walkway to the other. Add more sand as needed until the base is smooth.

7 Beginning at one corner of the walkway, lay the flagstones onto the sand base so the gap between stones is at least 3/8", but no more than 2". If needed, add or remove sand beneath stones to level them. Set the stones by tapping them with a rubber mallet or a length of 2 × 4.

8 Fill the gaps between stones with sand. (Use soil if you are planting grass or ground cover in the cracks.) Pack the sand with your fingers or a piece of scrap wood, then spray the walkway lightly with water to help the sand settle. Add new sand as necessary until gaps are filled.

How to Resurface a Sidewalk Using Mortared Brick Pavers

1 Select a paver pattern (page 51), then dig a trench around the concrete, slightly wider than the thickness of one paver. Dig the trench so it is about 3^1/$_2$" below the concrete surface. Soak the pavers with water before mortaring. Dry pavers absorb moisture, weakening the mortar strength.

2 Sweep the old concrete, then hose off the surface and sides with water to clear away dirt and debris. Mix a small batch of mortar according to manufacturer's directions. For convenience, place the mortar on a scrap of plywood.

3 Install edging bricks by applying a ^{1}/$_2$" layer of mortar to the side of the concrete slab and to one side of each brick. Set bricks into the trench, against the concrete. Brick edging should be ^{1}/$_2$" higher than the thickness of the brick pavers.

4 Finish the joints on the edging bricks with a V-shaped mortar tool (step 9), then mix and apply a ^{1}/$_2$"-thick bed of mortar to one end of the sidewalk, using a trowel. Mortar hardens very quickly, so work in sections no larger than 4 sq. ft.

5 Make a "screed" for smoothing mortar by notching the ends of a short 2 × 4 to fit between the edging bricks (page 39). Depth of the notches should equal the thickness of the pavers. Drag the screed across the mortar bed until the mortar is smooth.

6 Lay the paving bricks one at a time into the mortar, maintaining a 1/2" gap between pavers. (A piece of scrap plywood works well as a spacing guide.) Set the pavers by tapping them lightly with a rubber mallet.

7 As each section of pavers is completed, check with a straightedge to make sure the tops of the pavers are even.

8 When all the pavers are installed, use a mortar bag to fill the joints between the pavers with fresh mortar. Work in 4-sq.-ft. sections, and avoid getting mortar on the tops of the pavers.

9 Use a V-shaped mortar tool to finish the joints as you complete each 4-sq.-ft. section. For best results, finish the longer joints first, then the shorter joints. Use a trowel to remove excess mortar.

10 Let the mortar dry for a few hours, then scrub the pavers with a coarse rag and water. Cover the walkway with plastic and let the mortar cure for at least 24 hours. Remove plastic, but do not walk on the pavers for at least three days.

Simple garden steps can be built by making a series of concrete platforms framed with 5 × 6 timbers. Garden steps have shorter vertical risers and deeper horizontal treads than house stairs. Risers for garden stairs should be no more than 6", and treads should be at least 11" deep.

Building Garden Steps

Garden steps make sloping yards safer and more accessible. They also add visual interest by introducing new combinations of materials into your landscape design.

You can build garden steps with a wide variety of materials, including flagstone, brick, timbers, concrete block, or poured concrete. Whatever materials you use, make sure the steps are level and firmly anchored. They should be easy to climb and have a rough texture for good traction.

Everything You Need:

Tools: chain saw or reciprocating saw with 12" wood-cutting blade, tape measure, level, masonry hammer, shovel, drill with 1" spade bit and bit extension, rake, wheelbarrow, hoe, concrete float, edging tool, stiff brush.

Materials: 2 × 4 lumber, 5 × 6 landscape timbers, mason's string, 3/4" I.D. (interior diameter) black pipe, 12" galvanized spikes, premixed concrete, compactible gravel subbase, seed gravel, (1/2" maximum diameter), sheet plastic, burlap.

Tips for Mixing Concrete

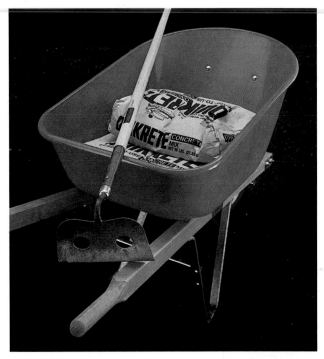

For large amounts (more than $1/2$ cubic yard), mix your own dry ingredients in a wheelbarrow or rented mixer. Use a ratio of 1 part portland cement (A), 2 parts sand (B), and 3 parts gravel (C). See page 5 to estimate the amount of concrete needed.

For small amounts (less than $1/2$ cubic yard), buy premixed bags of dry concrete. A 60-lb. bag of concrete creates about $1/2$ cubic foot of concrete. A special hoe with holes in the blade is useful for mixing concrete.

Tips for Building Garden Steps

1/8" downward pitch per foot

Build a slight downward pitch into outdoor steps so water will drain off without puddling. Do not exceed a pitch of $1/8$" per foot.

Order custom-cut timbers to reduce installation time if the dimensions of each step are identical. Some building supply centers charge a small fee for custom-cutting timbers.

How to Plan Garden Steps

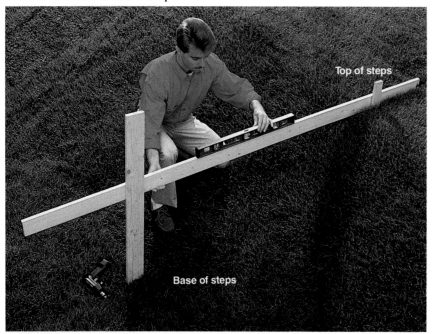

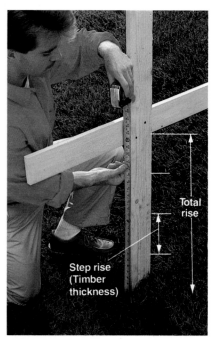

1 Drive a tall stake into the ground at the base of the stairway site. Adjust the stake so it is exactly plumb. Drive a shorter stake at the top of the site. Position a long, straight 2 × 4 against the stakes, with one end touching the ground next to the top stake. Adjust the 2 × 4 so it is level, then attach it to the stakes with screws. (For long spans, use a mason's string instead of a 2 × 4.)

2 Measure from the ground to the bottom of the 2 × 4 to find the total vertical **rise** of the stairway. Divide the rise by the actual thickness of the timbers (6" if using 5 × 6 timbers) to find the number of steps required. Round off fractions to the nearest full number.

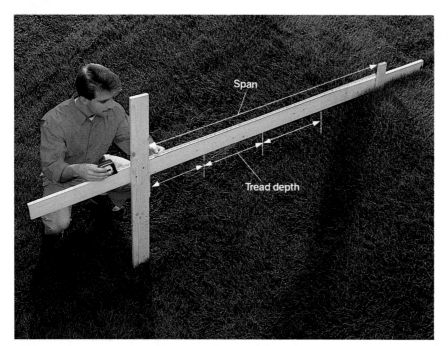

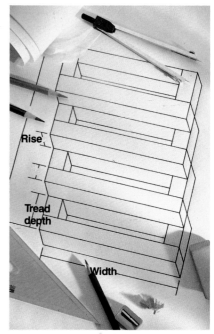

3 Measure along the 2 × 4 between the stakes to find the total horizontal **span**. Divide the span by the number of steps to find the depth of each step tread. If depth is less than 11", revise the step layout to extend the depth of the step treads.

4 Make a sketch of the step site, showing rise, tread depth, and width of each step. Remember that actual timber dimensions may vary from the nominal measurements.

1 Mark the sides of the step site with stakes and string. The stakes should be positioned at the front edge of the bottom step and the back edge of the top step.

2 Add the width of a timber (5") to the tread depth, then measure back this distance from the stakes and drive additional stakes to mark the back edge of the first step. Connect these stakes with string to mark the digging area for the first step.

3 Excavate for the first step, creating a flat bed with a very slight forward slope, no more than 1/8" from back to front. Front of excavation should be no more than 2" deep. Tamp the soil firmly.

4 For each step, use a chain saw or reciprocating saw to cut a front timber equal to the step width, a back timber 10" shorter, and two side timbers equal to the tread depth.

(continued next page)

5 Arrange the timbers to form the step frame, and end-nail them together with 12" spikes.

6 Set the timber frame in position. Use a carpenter's square to make sure the frame is square, and adjust as necessary. Drill two 1" guide holes in the front timber and the back timber, 1 ft. from the ends, using a spade bit and bit extension.

7 Anchor the steps to the ground by driving a 2 1/2- ft. length of 3/4" pipe through each guide hole until the pipe is flush with the timber. When pipes are driven, make sure the frame is level from side to side and has the proper forward pitch. Excavate for the next step, making sure the bottom of the excavation is even with top edge of the installed timbers.

Drive pipes here

8 Build another step frame and position it in the excavation so the front timber is directly over the rear timber on the first frame. Nail the steps together with three 12" spikes, then drill guide holes and drive two pipes through only the back timber to anchor the second frame.

9 Continue digging and installing the remaining frames until the steps reach full height. The back of the last step should be at ground level.

10 Staple plastic over the timbers to protect them from wet concrete. Cut away the plastic so it does not overhang into the frame opening.

11 Pour a 2" layer of compactible gravel subbase into each frame, and use a 2 × 4 to smooth it out.

12 Mix concrete in a wheelbarrow, adding just enough water so the concrete holds its shape when sliced with a trowel. NOTE: To save time and labor, you can have ready-mix concrete delivered to the site. Ready-mix companies will deliver concrete in amounts as small as 1/3 cubic yard (enough for three steps of the type shown here).

13 Shovel concrete into the bottom frame, flush with the top of the timbers. Work the concrete lightly with a garden rake to help remove air bubbles, but do not overwork the concrete.

(continued next page)

14 Smooth (screed) the concrete by dragging a 2 x 4 across the top of the frame. If necessary, add concrete to low areas and screed again until the surface is smooth and free of low spots.

15 While the concrete is still wet, "seed" it by scattering mixed gravel onto the surface. Sand-and-gravel suppliers and garden centers sell colorful gravel designed for seeding. For best results, select a mixture with stones no larger than 1/2" in diameter.

16 Press the seeded gravel into the surface of the concrete, using a concrete float, until the tops of the stones are flush with the surface of the concrete. Remove any concrete that spills over the edges of the frame, using a trowel.

17 Pour concrete into remaining steps, screeding and seeding each step before moving on to the next. For a neater appearance, use an edging tool (inset) to smooth the cracks between the timbers and the concrete as each step is finished.

18 When the sheen disappears from the poured concrete (4 to 6 hours after pouring), use a float to smooth out any high or low spots in each step. Be careful not to force seeded gravel too far into the concrete. Let the concrete dry overnight.

19 After concrete has dried overnight, apply a fine mist of water to the surface, then scrub it with a stiff brush to expose the seeded gravel.

VARIATION: To save time and money, skip the seeding procedure. To create a nonslip surface on smooth concrete, draw a stiff-bristled brush or broom once across the concrete while it is still wet.

20 Remove the plastic from the timbers, and cover the concrete with burlap. Allow concrete to cure for several days, spraying it occasionally with water to ensure even curing. NOTE: Concrete residue can be cleaned from timbers, using a solution of 5% muriatic acid and water.

Building a Patio

A patio can serve as the visual centerpiece of your yard and as the focus of your outdoor life-style. To be functional, a patio should be as large as a standard room—100 square feet or more.

Brick pavers are the most common material used for patios, but you can also build a patio with flagstone, following the same methods used for flagstone walkways (pages 34 to 41).

The most important part of a patio project is excavating and creating a flat base with the proper slope for drainage. This work is easier if you build your patio on a site that is relatively flat and level. On a hilly, uneven yard, you may be able to create flat space for a patio by building a retaining wall terrace (pages 16 to 25).

Everything You Need

Tools: tape measure, carpenter's level, shovel, line level, rake, hand tamper, tamping machine.

Materials: stakes, mason's string, compactible gravel subbase, rigid plastic edging, landscape fabric, sand, pavers, 1"-thick pipes.

Interlocking brick pavers come in many shapes and colors. Two popular paver styles include Uni-Decor™ (left) and Symmetry™ (right). Patios made with interlocking pavers may have a border row made from standard brick pavers (page opposite).

Common Paving Patterns for Standard Brick Pavers

Standard brick pavers can be arranged in several different patterns, including: (A) running bond, (B) jack-on-jack, (C) herringbone, and (D) basketweave. Jack-on-jack and basketweave patterns require fewer cut pavers along the edges. Standard pavers have spacing lugs on the sides that automatically set the joints at $1/8$" width. See page 5 to estimate the number of pavers you will need for your patio.

Installation Variations for Brick Pavers

Sand-set: Pavers rest on a 1" bed of sand laid over a 4" compactible gravel subbase. Rigid plastic edging holds the sand base in place. Joints are $1/8$" wide, and are packed with sand, which holds the pavers securely yet allows them to shift slightly as temperatures change.

Dry mortar: Installation is similar to sand-set patio, but joints are $3/8$" wide, and are packed with a mixture of sand and mortar, soaked with water, and finished with a V-shaped mortar tool. A dry-mortar patio has a more finished masonry look than a sand-set patio, but the joints must be repaired periodically.

Wet mortar: This method often is used when pavers are installed over an old concrete patio or sidewalk (see pages 40 to 41). Joints are $1/2$" wide. Wet mortar installation can also be used with flagstone. For edging on a wet-mortar patio, use rigid plastic edging or paver bricks set on end.

How to Build a Sand-set Patio with Brick Pavers

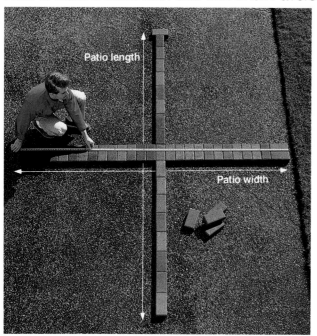

1 To find exact patio measurements and reduce the number of cut bricks needed, test-fit perpendicular rows of brick pavers on a flat surface, like a driveway. Lay two rows to reach the rough length and width of your patio, then measure the rows to find the exact size. (For a dry-mortar patio, put 3/8" spaces between pavers when test-fitting the rows.)

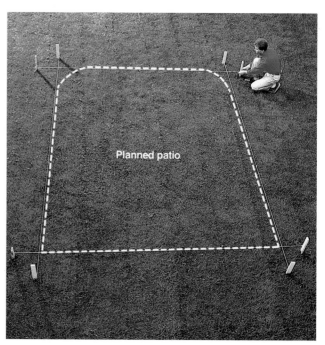

2 Use stakes and mason's string to mark out a rectangle that matches the length and width of your patio. Drive the stakes so they are at least 1 ft. outside the site of the planned patio. The intersecting strings mark the actual corners of the patio site.

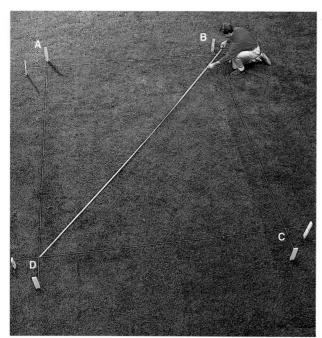

3 Check the rectangle for squareness by measuring the diagonals (A-C, B-D). If the rectangle is square, the diagonals will have the same measurement. If not, adjust the stakes and strings until the diagonals are equal. The strings will serve as a reference for excavating the patio site.

4 Using a line level as a guide, adjust one of the strings until it is level. When the string is level, mark its height on the stakes at each end of the string.

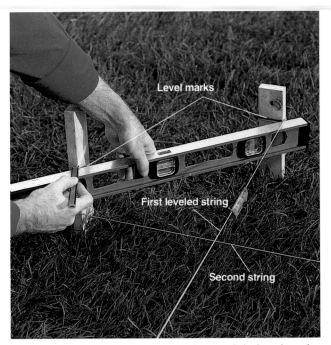

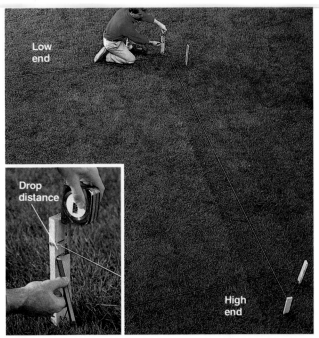

5 To adjust each remaining string so it is level and even with the first string, use a carpenter's level as a guide for marking adjacent stakes, then adjust the strings to the reference marks. Use a line level to make sure all strings are level.

6 To ensure good drainage, choose one end of the patio as the low end. (For most patios, this will be the end farthest from the house.) Measure from the high end to the low end (in feet), then multiply this number by 1/8" to find the proper drop distance. Measure down from the level marks on the low-end stakes, and mark the drop distance (inset).

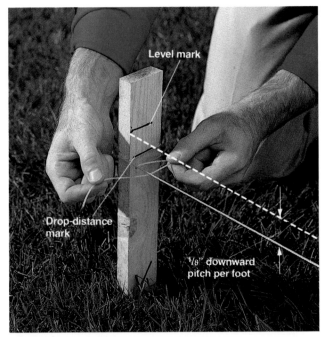

7 Lower the strings at the low-end stakes so the strings are even with the drop-distance marks. Keep all strings in place as a guide while excavating the site and installing the edging.

8 Remove all sod inside the strings and 6" beyond the edges of the planned patio. NOTE: If your patio will have rounded corners, use a garden hose or rope to outline the excavation.

(continued next page)

How to Build a Sand-set Patio with Brick Pavers (continued)

9 Starting at the outside edge, excavate the patio site so it is at least 5" deeper than the thickness of the pavers. For example, if your pavers are 1 3/4" thick, excavate to a depth of 6 3/4". Try to follow the slope of the side strings, and periodically use a long 2 × 4 to check the bottom of the excavation site for high and low spots.

10 Pour compactible gravel subbase over the patio site, then rake it into a smooth layer at least 4" deep. The thickness of the subbase layer may vary to compensate for unevenness in the excavation. Use a long 2 × 4 to check the surface of the subbase for high and low spots, and add or remove compactible gravel as needed.

11 Pack the subbase using a tamping machine until the surface is firm and flat. Check the slope of the subbase by measuring down from the side strings (see step 14). The space between the strings and the subbase should be equal at all points.

12 Cut strips of landscape fabric and lay them over the subbase to prevent weeds from growing up through the patio. Make sure the strips overlap by at least 6".

13 Install rigid plastic edging around the edges of the patio below the reference strings. Anchor the edging by driving galvanized spikes through the predrilled holes and into the subbase. To allow for possible adjustments, drive only enough spikes to keep the edging in place.

14 Check the slope by measuring from the string to the top of the edging at several points. The measurement should be the same at each point. If not, adjust the edging by adding or removing subbase material under the landscape fabric until the edging follows the slope of the strings.

15 For curves and rounded patio corners, use rigid plastic edging with notches on the outside flange. It may be necessary to anchor each section of edging with spikes to hold curved edging in place.

16 Remove the reference strings, then set 1"-thick pipes or wood strips across the patio area, spaced every 6 ft., to serve as depth spacers for laying the sand base.

(continued next page)

17 Lay a 1"-thick layer of sand over the landscape fabric and smooth it out with a garden rake. Sand should just cover the tops of the depth spacers.

18 Water the sand thoroughly, and pack it lightly with a hand tamper.

19 Screed the sand to an even layer by resting a long 2 × 4 on the spacers embedded in the sand and drawing the 2 × 4 across the spacers using a sawing motion. Add extra sand to fill footprints and low areas, then water, tamp, and screed the sand again until it is smooth and firmly packed.

20 Remove the embedded spacers along the sides of the patio base, then fill the grooves with sand and pat them smooth with the hand tamper.

21 Lay the first border paver in one corner of the patio. Make sure the paver rests firmly against the rigid plastic edging.

22 Lay the next border paver so it is tight against the previous paver. Set the pavers by tapping them into the sand with a mallet. Use the depth of the first paver as a guide for setting the remaining pavers.

23 Working outward from the corner, install 2-ft.-wide sections of border pavers and interior pavers, following the desired pattern. Keep the joints between pavers very tight. Set each paver by tapping it with the mallet.

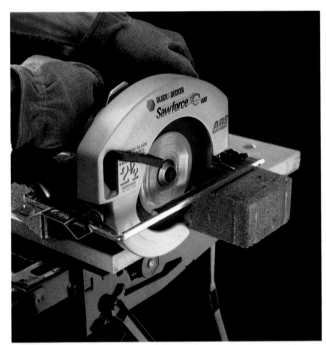

24 If your patio pattern requires that you cut pavers, use a circular saw with a diamond-tipped blade or masonry blade to saw them to size. Always wear eye protection and work gloves when cutting pavers.

25 After each section of pavers is set, use a straightedge to make sure the pavers are flat. Make adjustments by tapping high pavers deeper into the sand, or by removing low pavers and adding a thin layer of extra sand underneath them.

(continued next page)

26 Remove the remaining spacers when the installed surface gets near to them. Fill the gaps left by the spacers with loose sand, and pat the surface smooth with a hand tamper (inset).

27 Continue installing 2-ft.-wide sections of border pavers and interior pavers. As you approach the opposite side of the patio, reposition the rigid plastic edging, if necessary, so full-sized pavers will fit without cutting.

28 At rounded corners and curves, install border pavers in a fan pattern with even gaps between the pavers. Gentle curves may accommodate full-sized border pavers, but for sharper bends you may need to mark and trim wedge-shaped border pavers to make them fit.

29 Lay the remaining interior pavers. Where partial pavers are needed, hold a paver over the gap, and mark the cut with a pencil and straightedge. Cut pavers with a circular saw and masonry blade (step 24). After all pavers are installed, drive in the remaining edging spikes and pack soil behind the edging.

30 Use a long 2 × 4 to check the entire patio for flatness. Adjust uneven pavers by tapping high pavers deeper into the sand, or by removing low pavers and adding a thin layer of extra sand underneath them. After adjusting bricks, use a mason's string to check the rows for straightness.

31 Spread a 1/2" layer of sand over the patio. Use the tamping machine to compress the entire patio and pack sand into the joints.

32 Sweep up the loose sand, then soak the patio area thoroughly to settle the sand in the joints. Let the surface dry completely. If necessary, repeat step 31 until the gaps between pavers are packed tightly with sand.

Dry-mortar option: For a finished masonry look, install pavers with a 3/8" gap between bricks. Instead of sand, fill gaps with a dry mixture made from 4 parts sand and 1 part dry mortar. After spreading the dry mixture and tamping the patio, sprinkle surface with water. While mortar joints are damp, finish them with a V-shaped mortar tool (shown above). After mortar hardens, scrub pavers with water and a coarse rag.

Building a Wood Fence

A fence is as much a part of the neighborhood's landscape as your own. For this reason, local Building Codes and neighborhood covenants may restrict how and where you can build a fence.

In residential areas, for example, privacy fences usually are limited to 6 ft. in height. Remember that the fence you build to give you privacy also will obstruct the view of neighbors. Avoid hard feelings by discussing your plans with neighbors before building a fence. If you are willing to compromise, you may find that neighbors will share the work and expense.

Determine the exact property boundaries before you lay out the fence lines. You may need to call the city or county surveyor to pinpoint these boundaries. To avoid disputes, position your fence at least 6" inside the property line, even if there are no setback regulations.

To ensure sturdy construction, all screening fences should have posts anchored with concrete footings. When buying posts. remember that footing depths are determined by your local

Building Code. In cold climates, local Codes may require that fence footings extend past the winter frost line.

Many homes have chain-link fences that provide security but are not very attractive. To soften the look of chain-link, plant climbing vines, shrubs, or tall perennials against the fence.

Everything You Need:

Tools: tape measure, line level, plumb bob, rented power auger, circular saw, pencil, shovel, hammer, cordless screwdriver, paint brush, pressure sprayer.

Materials: 4 x 4 fence posts, stakes, mason's string, masking tape, coarse gravel, 2 x 4 lumber, premixed concrete, fence panels or boards, galvanized fence brackets, 4d galvanized nails, 3" galvanized utility screws, preassembled gate, gate hinges and latch, post caps, galvanized casing nails, liquid sealer-preservative.

A panel fence is easy to build, and is well suited for yards that are flat or that have a steady, gradual slope. On a sloped lot, install the panels in a step pattern, trying to keep an even vertical drop between panels. It is difficult to cut most preassembled panels, so try to plan the layout so only full-width panels are used. See pages 62 to 65.

A low fence establishes boundaries and adds to the landscape design, but it does not block your view completely. Low fences work well for confining children or pets.

A split-rail fence is an inexpensive, easy-to-build alternative that complements rustic, informal landscapes. Building centers stock precut cedar rails and posts for split-rail fences.

A board-and-stringer fence is made with individually cut pieces of lumber. A board-and-stringer fence is a good choice if preassembled panels are unavailable, or if your yard has steep or irregular slopes. See pages 66 to 67.

How to Install Fence Posts

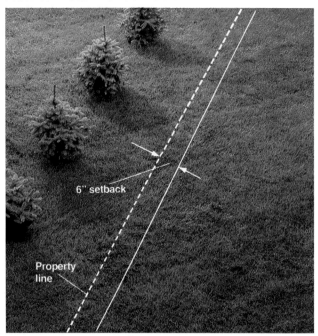

1 Determine the exact property lines if your fence will adjoin your neighbor's property. Plan your fence line with a setback of at least 6" from the legal property line. (Local regulations may require a larger setback.)

2 Mark the fence line with stakes and mason's string. Using a line level as a guide, adjust the string until it is level.

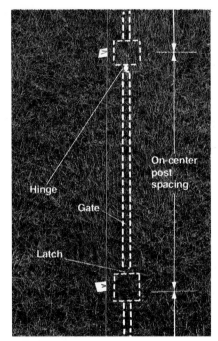

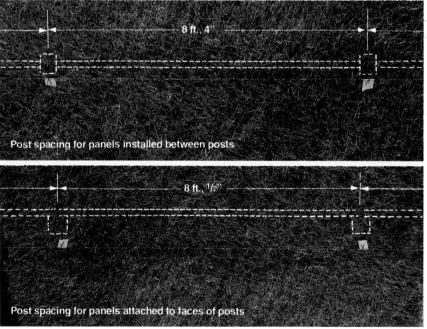

Post spacing for panels installed between posts

Post spacing for panels attached to faces of posts

3 Use masking tape to mark the string where the gate posts will be installed. Measure gate width, including hinges and latch hardware, then add 4" to find the on-center spacing between posts.

4 Mark string at remaining post locations. For a panel fence, try to plan the layout so cut panels will not be needed. If your fence will use 8-ft-long panels installed between 4 × 4 posts, space the posts 8 ft., 4" apart, on-center (top). If panels will be attached to faces of posts, space the posts 8 ft., 1/2" apart, on-center (bottom). For a custom board-and-stringer fence, posts can be set closer together for greater strength.

5 Use a plumb bob to pinpoint the post locations on the ground, then mark the locations with stakes and remove the string.

6 Dig post holes with a power auger, available at rental centers. Holes should be 6" deeper than the post footing depth specified by your local Building Code. Pour a 6" layer of gravel into each hole to improve drainage.

7 Position each post in its hole. Adjust the post until it is plumb, then brace it with scrap pieces of 2 × 4 driven into the ground and screwed to the sides of the post.

8 When all posts are in position, use the mason's string to make sure the fence line is straight. Adjust the posts, if necessary, until the fence line is straight and the posts are plumb.

9 Fill each post hole with premixed concrete. Overfill the holes slightly. Check posts to make sure they are plumb, then shape the concrete around the bottom of each post to form a rounded crown that will shed water (inset). Let concrete cure for 48 hours before continuing with fence construction.

How to Install Preassembled Fence Panels

1 After posts are installed (pages 62 to 63), test-fit the panels and gates to make sure they fit between the posts. If necessary, trim the edges of the panels slightly to improve the fit (inset).

2 Mark the position of fence panels on the sides of the posts. Make sure the bottom of the panels will be at least 2" above ground level. On level sites, use a line level to ensure that the outlines are at the same level. On a sloped site where panels will be installed step-fashion, try to maintain a uniform vertical drop with each panel.

3 Attach three evenly spaced fence brackets inside each drawn outline on the sides of the posts, using 4d galvanized nails. The bottom bracket should be aligned against the bottom of the outline (inset). On the top two brackets, bend the bottom flange flat against the post. See VARIATION (next page) if panels will be attached to the front faces of the posts.

4 Slide the fence panels into the brackets from above until they rest on the bottom flanges of the lowest brackets. Attach the panels from each side by driving 4d galvanized nails through the holes in the brackets (inset). NOTE: To provide easy access for delivering furniture or other large materials through your yard, attach one fence panel with screws so it can be removed easily.

VARIATION: To attach panels to the front faces of posts, position each panel so it is level, then anchor it by driving galvanized utility screws through panel frames and into the posts. Space the screws 18" apart.

5 Attach three evenly spaced hinges to the gate frame, using galvanized screws. Follow the hardware manufacturer's directions, making sure the hinge pins are straight and parallel with the edge of the gate.

6 Position the gate between the gate posts so the hinge pins rest against one post. Set the gate on wood blocks, then attach the hinges to the post with galvanized screws.

7 Attach the latch hardware to the other gate post and to the gate, using galvanized screws. Open and close the gate to make sure the latch works correctly.

8 Measure and trim the tops of the posts to a uniform height, using a reciprocating saw or hand-saw. (If you are not using post caps, cut the posts to a point to help them shed water.)

9 Cover flat post tops with decorative wood or metal caps, and attach them with galvanized casing nails. Coat the fence with sealer-preservative or paint.

How to Build a Fence Using Boards & Stringers

1 Install fence posts (pages 62 to 63). Mark cutoff lines on the end posts, 1 ft. below the planned height of the finished fence, then attach a chalk line to the height marks on the end posts, and snap a cutoff line across the posts. (Board-and-stringer fences usually are constructed so the vertical boards extend above the posts.)

2 Trim off the posts along the marked cutoff lines, using a reciprocating saw or handsaw. Brush sealer-preservative onto the cut ends of the posts.

3 Cut 2 × 4 top stringers and coat the ends with sealer-preservative. Center the end joints over the posts, then attach the stringers to the posts with galvanized screws or nails.

4 Mark lines on each post to serve as references for installing additional stringers. Space the marks at 2-ft. intervals.

5 At each stringer reference mark, use galvanized nails to attach a 2" fence bracket to the sides of the posts. Brackets should be flush with the front face of the posts.

6 Position a 2 × 4 stringer between each pair of fence brackets. Hold or tack the stringer against the posts, then mark it for cutting by marking back side along the edges of posts. (If yard is sloped, stringers will be cut at angles.) Cut stringers 1/4" shorter than measurement so stringer will slide into brackets easily.

7 Slide the stringers into the fence brackets and attach them with galvanized nails. If stringers are cut at an angle because of the ground slope, bend the bottom flanges on the fence brackets to match this angle before installing the stringers.

8 Install vertical boards, beginning at an end post. To find board length, measure from the ground to the top edge of the top stringer, then add 10". Cut board to length, then use galvanized screws to attach it to post or rails. Boards should be plumb, and should extend 1 ft. above the top stringer, leaving a 2" gap at the bottom.

9 Measure and cut the remaining fence boards, and attach them to the stringers with galvanized screws. Leave a gap of at least 1/8" between boards (a piece of scrap wood works well as a spacing guide). Each board should extend exactly 1 ft. above the top stringer, and should have a 2" gap at the bottom. At the corners and ends of the fence, you may need to rip-cut fence boards to make them fit.

10 Attach a prebuilt gate as shown on page 65. Finish the fence by coating it with sealer-preservative or paint.

Building Garden Ponds

Garden ponds provide a focal point and create a feeling of serenity in any yard. Ponds also expand your planting options and attract new, unusual species of wildlife.

Modern materials have simplified pond-building and made ponds more affordable. Expensive pumps and filtration systems usually are not necessary in small ponds, although they do enable the pond to support more plants and fish.

Artificial garden ponds require pond liners, which are available in two basic types: liner shells and flexible liners. Fiberglass liner shells are easy to install—simply dig a hole and set them in the ground. They are inexpensive and available in many shapes and sizes, but they may crack in very cold weather.

Most garden ponds are built with soft, flexible liners that conform to any shape and size. Some flexible liners are made from polyvinyl chloride (PVC) fabric. PVC liners are economical, but they can become brittle in just a few years.

Better-quality flexible pond liners are made of rubber. Rubber liners are more costly, but also more durable than PVC liners or fiberglass shells.

Everything You Need:

Tools: hose, garden spade, carpenter's level, hand spade or trowel.

Materials: pond liner, sand, mortar mix, flagstone coping stones, long 2 × 4.

Sizing Chart for Flexible Liners		
Liner Size	Maximum Pond Size	
	18" deep	24" deep
8 × 10	4 × 6	3 × 5
10 × 10	6 × 6	5 × 5
10 × 15	6 × 11	5 × 10
15 × 15	11 × 11	10 × 10

Flexible pond liners (above) adapt to nearly any shape or size you want. A shallow shelf holds potted plants. **Fiberglass liner shells** (below) come in many sizes and shapes. Simply set them in the ground and they are ready to stock with fish and aquatic plants.

Photo by Susan Roth

Select a level site for your garden pond. Sloping ground requires a lot of digging and does not provide a natural setting for the pond. Do not build a pond directly under a tree, since fallen leaves contaminate water and root systems make digging difficult. Ponds should not receive too much direct sunshine, however, so choose a site that is in the shadow of a tree or another landscape structure for at least half the day.

Replenish water supply regularly, especially during hot, dry weather. Ponds stocked only with hardy aquatic plants may be replenished with tap water from a garden hose. If the pond is stocked with fish, let water sit for at least three days so chlorine can evaporate before the water is added to the pond.

Collect rainwater in a barrel to replenish ponds that are stocked with fish or very delicate plants. Rainwater is preferable to city water, which contains chemical additives, like chlorine.

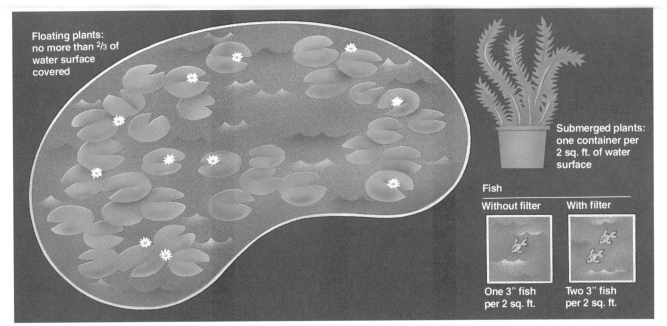

Floating plants: no more than ⅔ of water surface covered

Submerged plants: one container per 2 sq. ft. of water surface

Fish

Without filter	With filter
One 3" fish per 2 sq. ft.	Two 3" fish per 2 sq. ft.

Keep a balance of plants and fish in your pond. Floating plants provide shade for fish and help inhibit algae, but should cover no more than ⅔ of the pond surface. Every pond should have at least one container of submerged plants, which provide oxygen for fish, for every two square feet of pond surface. (NOTE: aquatic plants are available at local nurseries or from mail-order suppliers. Taking aquatic plants from lakes and ponds is illegal in most areas.) Fish add interest to your pond and release carbon dioxide that can be used by plants. Stock no more than one 3" fish per two square feet of surface if your pond does not have an aeration and filtration system. After filling the pond, let water sit for at least one week before stocking it with plants and fish. Ponds with fish should be at least 24" deep.

Planter shown cutaway

Plastic planter

Aquarium gravel

Topsoil

Landscape fabric

1" holes

Build containers for aquatic plants by drilling 1" holes in plastic planters and lining them with landscape fabric. Holes allow water to circulate past the roots of the plants. Planters protect pond liners and simplify maintenance.

Use chemicals sparingly. Little maintenance other than a yearly cleaning is needed for balanced ponds. Water-quality problems, like algae buildup, can be treated with diluted chemical products sold in pet stores.

Bring plants and fish indoors if your pond freezes for more than a week or two during the winter. Cut away plant stems, then store the plants in a dry, dark location. Keep fish in an aerated aquarium during long periods of freezing weather.

How to Install a Garden Pond with a Flexible Liner

1 Select a site for the pond (see page 70) and outline the pond with a hose or heavy rope. Avoid sharp angles, corners, and symmetrical shapes. Ponds should have at least 15 square feet of surface area. Minimum depth is 18" for plants only, and 24" if fish will be added to the pond.

2 Excavate the entire pond area to a depth of about 1 ft. The sides of the pond should slope slightly toward the center. Save some of the topsoil for use with aquatic plants (page 71).

3 Excavate the center of the pond to maximum depth, plus 2" to allow for a layer of sand. Leave a 1-ft.-wide shelf inside the border to hold aquatic planters. The pond bed should be flat, with walls sloping downward from the shelf.

4 Lay a straight board across the pond, then place a carpenter's level on the board. Check all sides to make sure the edges of the pond are level. If not, adjust the surrounding ground to level by digging, filling, and packing soil.

5 Once the excavation is completed and the site is level, dig a shallow bed around the perimeter of the pond to hold the border flagstones (called coping stones).

6 Remove all stones, roots, and sharp objects from the pond bed, then smooth out the soil base. Next, spread a 2" layer of wet sand on the level areas of the pond bed. Pack the sand with a tamper, then smooth it out with a length of 2 × 4.

OPTION: When using the more inexpensive (and more fragile) PVC pond liners, line the hole with cardboard or old carpeting pieces before installing the liner. The protective layer helps prevent puncturing and stretching of the liner.

7 Place the liner into the pond bed, then fold and tuck the liner so it conforms to the shape of the hole. Smooth out the liner as much as possible, avoiding any sharp creases.

(continued next page)

How to Install a Garden Pond with a Flexible Liner (continued)

8 Set a few stones on the overhang to hold the liner in place. Too many stones will cause the liner to stretch, not settle into the hole, when it is filled with water.

9 Fill the pond up to the top with water. Smooth out any large creases or wrinkles that develop as the water level rises. Remove the stones after the pond is full, and allow the liner to settle for one day.

10 Using a scissors, trim the liner so it overhangs the top of the pond by about 12" all the way around the perimeter of the pond.

11 Spread a mixture of 20 parts sand to one part dry mortar in a shallow layer on top of the liner overhang. Spray with a light mist. Set coping stones into the sand so they overhang the edge of the pond by about 2". Set one of the stones ½" lower than the rest, to serve as an overflow point for excess water.

How to Install a Garden Pond with a Liner Shell

1 Set the fiberglass liner shell in place, then use ropes to outline both the flat bottom and the outside edge of the liner on the ground. Use a level to make sure the outline is directly below the outside edge of the shell.

2 Excavate the center of the site to maximum shell depth, then excavate the sides so they slope inward to the flat bottom. Test-fit the shell repeatedly, digging and filling until the shape of the hole matches the shell.

3 Remove all stones and sharp objects, then set the shell into the hole. Check with a level to make sure the shell is level, and adjust the hole as necessary. The top of the shell should be slightly above ground level.

4 Begin slowly filling the shell with water. As the water level rises, pack wet sand into any gaps between the shell and the sides of the hole.

5 Dig a shallow bed around the perimeter of the liner to hold coping stones, if desired. Place the stones near the pond liner, but do not set them on the liner edges. Any weight on the edges of fiberglass shell could cause it to crack.

Creating a Planting Area

Planting areas provide a natural finishing touch to a landscape. A planting area can hold an elaborate bed of flowers, a vegetable garden, a group of ornamental trees, or a simple shrub surrounded by a bed of gravel or bark chips. Retaining wall materials (pages 16 to 25) often are used to make raised or terraced planting areas.

Make your planting areas proportionate to your yard size. Some landscape designers advise that planting areas should occupy at least 50% of the total yard space.

Unless your soil is very rich, you probably will need to add fertilizer, peat moss, or mulch to make it more suitable for planting. The type of soil builders you add depends on the quality of your soil and the kinds of plants you want to grow. To find the best soil builders, take a sample of your soil to a local garden center or a university extension service for a soil analysis.

Use edgings around planting areas to define borders and reduce maintenance. Without edgings, lawn grass will spread into your planting area and loose-fill materials can spill out. The flexible plastic edging shown above is inexpensive and easy to install. Other edging options are shown below.

Everything You Need:

Tools: hose, shovel, garden rake, scissors, hand spade.

Materials: see photos below.

Materials for Planting Areas

Common edging materials include: (A) standard brick pavers, (B) interlocking pavers set on edge, (C) cut-stone slabs, (D) rough stone, or (E) wood. To prevent weeds from sprouting, cover the planting area with landscape fabric (page 6) before planting, and cover the planting area with bark chips or another loose-fill material.

Natural soil builders improve the growing quality of soil without relying on hazardous chemicals. Composted manure is a mild, slow-release fertilizer ideal for all plants. Peat moss makes heavy, clay soil more workable, and it also neutralizes acidic or alkaline soil. Bone meal is high in phosphorus—an essential nutrient for fruits and vegetables.

How to Make a Planting Area

1 Outline the planting area, using a garden hose or rope. Cut away the existing lawn inside the outline to a depth of 3" to 4".

2 Dig a narrow trench around the sides of the cut-out area, and install the edging material so the top of the edging is just above ground level. Join the ends of flexible plastic edging with a plastic connector. Pack soil around the edging to hold it in place.

3 Spread any necessary soil builders over the planting area. Use a shovel to loosen soil 12" deep and work the soil builders into the ground.

4 Rake the surface smooth, and remove any rocks, sticks, and roots.

5 Lay landscape fabric over the planting area, and trim away the edges with a scissors. Cut X-shaped slits in the fabric where each plant will be located, and dig a planting hole in the soil below.

6 Transplant flowers from their containers to the planting area, then lay an even layer of loose-fill mulch over the landscape fabric and around the base of each plant. Water the area thoroughly.

Maintaining a Landscape

Like the other areas of your home, your finished yard requires periodic maintenance. But most do-it-yourself home landscapers soon find that yard work is more like an enjoyable hobby than a tiresome chore. Watching your landscape mature and planning new projects is all the more enjoyable when the landscape was built by your own hands.

Keep a seasonal and weekly schedule for outdoor work. In addition to weekly mowing, watering, and weeding, plan on spending some time every two or three months to inspect and repair landscape structures and tend to the seasonal needs of plants. In particular, trees and shrubs need to be pruned occasionally to stimulate good growth.

Follow these simple maintenance tips to protect your landscape and ensure your continued enjoyment.

Protect wood structures by treating them every two or three years with sealer-preservative, stain, or exterior paint. Sealer-preservative can be applied with a pressure sprayer, but remember that these liquids are toxic. Take care not to breathe the vapors, and make sure the spray does not fall on living plants. Replace any rotted boards.

How to Maintain a Brick Paver Patio

1 Once a year, inspect the joints between the pavers, and remove any weeds, debris, or cracked mortar.

2 Refill the joints by packing them with fine sand or dry mortar mix. Sweep the patio thoroughly.

3 Seal the entire surface with liquid masonry sealer applied with a pressure sprayer. Sealers protect the pavers from water damage and prevent weeds from sprouting

Index

Creative Publishing International, Inc.
offers a variety of how-to books.
For information write:
Creative Publishing International, Inc.
Subscriber Books
5900 Green Oak Drive
Minnetonka, MN 55343